# THINK OF LAMPEDUSA

# African
# POETRY
## BOOK SERIES

Series editor: Kwame Dawes

# THINK OF LAMPEDUSA

*Josué Guébo*

Translated by Todd Fredson
Introduction by John Keene

*University of Nebraska Press / Lincoln and London*

Eleven poems and portions of the translator's note, "The Most
Dangerous Crossing: Reconstituting Nationality in Josué Guébo's *Songe
à Lampedusa*," appeared in *Blackbird: an online journal of literature
and the arts* 15 no. 2 (Fall 2016). Nine poems were introduced with
portions of the translator's note in *Boston Review* October 6, 2016.

The African Poetry Book Series has been made possible through the generosity
of philanthropists Laura and Robert F. X. Sillerman, whose contributions have
facilitated the establishment and operation of the African Poetry Book Fund.

Library of Congress Cataloging-in-Publication Data
Names: Guébo, Josué, 1972– author.
| Fredson, Todd, translator. | Keene,
John, 1965– writer of introduction.
Title: Think of Lampedusa / Josué Guébo; translated by
Todd Fredson; introduction by John Keene.
Other titles: Songe à Lampedusa. English
Description: Lincoln: University of Nebraska
Press, [2017] | Series: African poetry book |
Identifiers: LCCN 2017010481 (print)
LCCN 2017027867 (ebook)
ISBN 9781496200426 (paperback: alk. paper)
ISBN 9781496204714 (epub)
ISBN 9781496204721 (mobi)
ISBN 9781496204738 (pdf)
Subjects: | BISAC: POETRY / African.
Classification: LCC PQ3989.3.G77 (ebook) | LCC
PQ3989.3.G77 A2 2017 (print) | DDC 841/.92—dc23
LC record available at https://lccn.loc.gov/2017010481

Set in Garamond Premier by John Klopping.
Designed by N. Putens.

# CONTENTS

Introduction by John Keene  *vii*

Translator's Note  *xi*

Think of Lampedusa  *1*

Notes  *65*

# INTRODUCTION

*John Keene*


Throughout the first fifteen years of the twenty-first century, the increasing waves of refugees, particularly from the global South to Europe and North America, have focused public attention in the West on the issues of global displacement, dispossession, and migration. In the wake of neoliberal capitalism's global depredations, the United States–led wars in Afghanistan and Iraq, and numerous metastasizing domestic and international conflicts furthered by Western powers throughout the Middle East, Africa, and Asia, political, social, and economic refugees and migrants have headed for regions that they envision offer opportunities not only for survival but also which present the possibility of a livelihood and some measure of security. Europe, because of its comparative wealth, proximity to multiple regions in tumult, long colonial history, and—over the last half century—self-proclaimed adherence to liberal values and defense of human rights has been a primary destination for migrants, with the countries constituting its periphery, such as Italy, serving as the main and often deadly entry points.

It is this story writ large—and in particular one tragic, representative incident, the 2013 Lampedusa migrant shipwreck—that Ivorian academic, poet, short story writer, and intellectual Josué Guébo (born in 1972 in Abidjan, Ivory Coast) explores in his fifth book of poetry, *Think of Lampedusa*. Originally published in French in 2014, and translated into English with an expert hand by poet and critic Todd Fredson, Guébo's book and its title invoke the Sicilian island of Lampedusa. The largest in Italy's Pelagic chain, it constitutes the geographical and, in some ways, figurative and metaphysical southernmost edge of the European Union. Lampedusa also is the closest European point to the northern African nation of Libya, through which many thousands of migrants have passed on their way to various points in the European Union.

*Think of Lampedusa* comprises a long, untitled poem in more than four dozen untitled, single-stanza sections, each of similar length. It captures with mordant irony the mixture of utopian longing, pragmatic self-preservation, and brutal horror exacted by the psychic, physical, and spiritual journeys across the sea and into the void of unknowing that contemporary migration from the global South often represents. Guébo shows Lampedusa and Libya to be latter-day purgatories, way stations between life and death, bookending the watery grave into which hundreds of people from Eritrea, Somalia, and Ghana plunged on October 3, 2013, and where, only a few weeks later, nearly three dozen more migrants, from Eritrea and Somalia, sank to their deaths. Just as many others have died there before and since.

Guébo's poem, however, eschews the documentary in its style and effects, though it does at various points include concrete statistics about the human toll of migration. He does not present the direct voices, as individuated testimony, of those balancing hope and fear on the over-loaded boats and rafts nor does he tally the long list of countries where the refugees have come from or where they are heading, though one can summon both the likely origins and potential destinations from the last fifteen years' news reports. Guébo's approach, rather, represents a lyric of recording and witnessing that refracts multifarious, often tragic experience through an incisive, sometimes lamentative poetic speaker. His imagery is both fluid and fragmentary, held together by a flexible syntax, adroitly transferred into English by Fredson, that allows him to meld specificity and abstraction, placing the reader both within and outside any particular scene, be it a vessel plunging into the waters off Lampedusa's coasts or the interminable wait at an immigration checkpoint.

The poetic achievement and political resonance of *Think of Lampedusa*, which received the 2014 Tchicaya U Tam'si Prize, underscores Guébo's importance as one of the leading figures in Ivorian literature. In it one can see parallels not only with Guébo's major Ivorian peers, such as Tanella Boni, but with broader traditions in twentieth-century and contemporary African and Francophone poetry. It demonstrates his ongoing conversation with Ivorian predecessors like Bernard Dadié and, from a later generation, Véronique Tadjo, as well as a broader array of poets from across the continent and Diaspora—a group that might encompass U Tam'si himself, Aimé Césaire, Werewere Liking, Wole Soyinka, and Will Alexander.

In Guébo's citation of Lampedusa, one also hears echoes and sees a palimpsest of French painter Théodore Géricault's famous painting *The Raft of the Medusa* (1818–19), which depicted the horrific aftermath of the grounding of the French naval frigate *Méduse* off the Mauritanian coast, eventually resulting in the deaths of all but fifteen or so of its passengers. In Guébo's poem, certain conceptual elements in Géricault's work are reversed, with the black and brown voyagers heading to Lampedusa the ones falling prey to drowning and starvation. The French painter's portrait is drained of its colonial romanticism in favor of a sentiment approaching cynicism in its lapidary clarity about the reality the seafarers he is writing about have faced and are likely to meet in the future. As the poem's speaker says:

I'd reimagine that fire in the ship's hold
the seasonal suicide epidemic
I'd say happy the castaways
they will be naturalized
Happy absentees
the toasts they'll receive
Haven't they lifted the elbow of that anchor
drank to the bubbles of this dream
(p. 9)

Guébo underlines this allegorical sense of continuity between past and present, between the postcolonial subalterns in flight and the colonial, imperial, and local forces that have produced the societal disruptions leading to forced migration through a deft mixing of the real and mythical. In one stanza, the classical Greek hero Ulysses assumes the guises both of Soumaré Kanté, the thirteenth-century king of the Sasso people who was the subject of a Mandinka epic, and the controversial French comedian Dieudonné Mbala Mbala, the product of a black Cameroonian father and white French mother, recently banned for his repeated anti-Semitic comments but who remains a figure of resistance for many young first- and second-generation immigrant members of the French polity. Guébo's poem thereby opens avenues of interpretation, even as his empathy clearly lands on the side of those who have been dispossessed into flight, and his political position offers a critique of the conditions, including the civil war in his own country, that create such widespread social and political disruption.

In as much as Guébo captures the 2013 tragedy, the poem also remains prescient. A spate of migrant shipwrecks in 2014 and subsequent years, as well as the unfolding refugee crises that have commanded the attention of the news media over the last two years, point to the salience of *Think of Lampedusa*'s concern with a topic the West still struggles to understand, let alone adequately address. Yet Guébo is not without hope, even it if is contingent and ephemeral. Such is the power of words, of the imagination, of the human spirit itself, as he suggests:

At the back of the raft
I invent a city
dependable as a diurnal tale
A city that fills all of our hopes with the scent of lemon
We'd dream passionately about this city
The thirst of its travelers sticking in its long mane
On its docks one thousand workers
build the dreams they would step into
youthfully extravagant
(p. 61)

# TRANSLATOR'S NOTE

*Todd Fredson*

I have benefited from spending time with Josué Guébo. I mean that this translation has benefited from that time—several months of collaboration in the Ivory Coast—but also, I mean that I have personally benefited. My understanding of the complexities of the lives lived in the Ivory Coast, which has recently emerged from two civil wars (from 2002 to 2007 and in 2011) has deepened. My understanding of the lives lived in West Africa, in Africa, in former colonies, and in the crosshairs of a global economy built on (neo)colonial principles has deepened. My understanding is visceral. This conversion, whereby an intellectual understanding becomes a felt experience is, I would like to believe, also available for the reader encountering Guébo's work here in translation.

In *Think of Lampedusa*, Guébo immerses us in the wreckage along what has become the most dangerous migrant route in the world—from northern Africa to Europe by boat across the Mediterranean Sea. Crossing to the Italian island of Lampedusa, some seventy miles from Tunisia, is the shortest route. On October 3, 2013, 366 Africans died attempting to reach Lampedusa, a tragedy that provided a preview to the escalating migration crisis on the Mediterranean and the European Union's response to it.

Guébo's work here strikes me as a kind of surrealist form of docu-

mentary poetics. His dark, absurdist moments recall the French sur-
realists and their precursors, the French symbolists. Rimbaud's fever
dreams seem to linger atmospherically in these poems—and Guébo pays
homage to Paul Verlaine. "The long sobs of the violins of Autumn" in
Verlaine's "Autumn Song" become "the slow vessels carrying autumn's
violators." Guébo's poetry does not stylistically engage the social realism
that is conventionally associated with documentary poetics, but his
work unflinchingly confronts the colonial legacies and sociopolitical
circumstances that acutely impact daily life in the Ivory Coast, and in
Africa more broadly. Describing a previous collection, poet and editor
Paul Dakeyo characterizes Guébo's work as a "vibrant call to revisit
African history in order to better direct its people toward a new time
under the sun."[1] Guébo's call to aim Africans toward a new time under
the sun means that while he may not favor a realist aesthetic, the facts
of the matter—and even the statistics—must be reckoned with. As he
designs his imaginary for the 366 Africans killed at sea, for instance, he
thinks of the others who have died attempting this crossing to Europe:

> The battered hull would begin to unflap
> its beautiful mouth of statistics
> This sea of endemic wreckage
> Some cry seventeen thousand deaths in twenty years
> others only three thousand
> as if each corpse in this Mediterranean
> was not excessive
> (p. 33)

Guébo's historical attention, even when it is not rendered in such
precise terms, provides a purpose or an urgency that textures his poems.
His own history—the cultural, personal, and literary background that
situates him in relation to his subject—became available through our
conversations. This is the advantage of translating a living poet, partic-
ularly in the case of African poets because, except rarely, there is not a
support system of universities and libraries preserving the archives of

the authors' notes, drafts, letters, and other papers. Translating the work of West African poets, I have come to understand their writing reflexes, or some of the details that guide their writing decisions, *only* through conversations with the authors or with people who have known them.

Translators often talk about balancing what is gained and what is lost as a poem moves from one language to another—but can it be more than just a one-way journey? I think this is what Ngũgĩ wa Thiong'o has in mind when he proposes approaching translation as a kind of conversation: "Translation seen as conversation—for conversation assumes equality among the speakers—is clearly the language of languages, the language that all languages should speak."[2] This equality among speakers is a trust that the listener knows how to feel the textures of the received speech, and to incorporate them, and that the listener, who is the translator, will make a translation that is actually a reply, and which expands the conversation, inviting more people to it.

I think Ngũgĩ's proposal resonates with this text for three reasons. First, conversation is how the book was translated—many conversations across several months in Abidjan, in the Ivory Coast. Second, this aspiration that equality can be achieved between participants in a conversation resembles the hope of the people in this book who are migrating from one shore to another—who might hope to arrive on the European shore without having to dispossess themselves of their own histories, and who might hope that it is not a one-way journey. Third, though I have translated *Think of Lampedusa* from French, the book's imaginary evolved out of a conversation between at least two languages, Guébo's first language, Dida, and the French in which he writes. This is a work, in other words, that was fundamentally formed by a conversation between languages—it was a translation arrived at out of conversation even before I joined in, even before I made my reply in English.

In the vein of "what is lost" in translation, let me circulate a few more ideas that are part of the conversation I am having with Josué Guébo in this translation of *Think of Lampedusa*. This is an opportunity for me to account more completely for a gesture that he uses to lull and displace the reader, and ultimately to ferry his readers into an irresolvable space. Guébo's lines, which are lyric fragments, often refer backward and forward simultaneously, suspending the reader between possible meanings and readerly directions. No semantic destination clearly presents itself. The lines float and tether loosely:

> calling other pieces into confidence
> each word grabs the shoulder strap
> of the word to come
> (p. 17)

In this way, he maintains a connotative stance until a sequence of lines resolves itself. A scene emerges and an allegorical drama unfolds, often concluding in a surrealist flare. Here, language is heightened. It turns inward, as if toward the speaker's private idiom, and the reader is set adrift or submerged in the oceanic.

One such passage was particularly vexing to translate. As he completes a drama in which the speaker arrives to a market where friendship "instructs the one hand / to draw in the other of day" and where the solstices are shopping at the stalls, the speaker affirms that

> A new material would spin the cotton of new adventures
> and the language that it speaks
> would turn its maxims seven times in the palace of dawn
> (p. 57)

In French, this last line is not, perhaps, as hermetic as it feels in English. It is, still, highly idiomatic. Guébo welds a French proverb to an image that becomes thematically weighted over the course of the collection. The French proverb advises that it is prudent to turn the tongue seven times before offering an opinion. The equivalent in English might be "think before you speak." And "palace" is an established metaphor for the mouth, so that the maxims are mulled over here. Guébo affixes the "dawn," which adds another dimension. The "palace of dawn" hints that the mouth verges on opening. Throughout the collection, the image of dawn is developed to conceptualize an event horizon for Africa, a dialectical turn to which Dakeyo alludes in his assessment of Guébo's poetic mission. The maxims turned "seven times in the palace of dawn" suggest that, after long being silenced on the international scene, Africa is prepared with its insights.

It is difficult to strip the French proverb from the "palace" metaphor, which itself is then fully constituted by the trope of dawn. And while there are these external references in the French from which to work, I invited the heightened surrealist punctuation. I chose to let the power of the image stand, and, perhaps, to estrange or to arrest the reader.

Finally, let me add a note about the title. I've translated the title *Songe à Lampedusa* as *Think of Lampedusa* and would like to take this opportunity to nuance that translation. There are meanings for *songe* that will not otherwise appear. *Songe*, while it can mean "think," implies a certain kind of thinking. "Consider" would have been a viable alternative. Reading W. S. Merwin's translations of Jean Follain's poems in *Transparence of the World*, I see Merwin translating the adjectival form of *songer, songeuse*, as "pensive"—*sa toux songeuse*, "his pensive cough." *Songer* has this introspective quality, a dose of longing. *Songe* is the imperative form of *songer*, but Guébo has chosen the familiar imperative, *(tu) songe*, rather than the formal imperative, *(vous) songez*. He implores a singular "you," rather than a plural and more abstract "you," to think. Guébo imparts a quality of intimacy, of direct address, through this choice. "Dream" could also have worked as a translation, or "imagine." But not enough action is felt, not enough movement is connoted in "dream" or "imagine"—that's not the way those words resonate in American English, for me, anyway. Around the topic of immigration in the U.S. context, "dream" is attached to a narrative of futurity, a kind of reverie—too stagnant, too hypothetical. "Dream" is not concrete enough to include the material conditions that demand an immediate decision: do something. Travel country to country to country. Admittedly, this choice, "think" instead of "dream," may just betray my own pessimism about the contrast between the American Dream broadcast to the world and the reality of the United States' structural inequality, in which access to that dream—the promise of safety and upward mobility—is so stringently monitored.

You will see that I have used endnotes in this text. I take my cue from Guébo who, himself, in the original text, offered the translation of a Dida phrase in a footnote.

NOTES

1. Introduction to *Carnet de doute* (Dakar: Panafrika/Silex/Nouvelles du sud, 2011), quotation translated by Todd Fredson.
2. In the spirit of ongoing exchange, let me note that this quote from Ngũgĩ wa Thiong'o was supplied by Edith Grossman in her book, *Why Translation Matters*.

# THINK OF LAMPEDUSA

I will tell you for the last time
my history, my wave

I have dreamed of you
as one dreams of an eye
without an eyelid
A story alive within these nights
where I rest with my eyes peeled
My hope tangled
on these roadsides
I dreamed about you
like one dreams simply
of a hand
or of day
Light Dreamed
of morning
where the day relies
on the raft's flame
a flame in agreement
with all these hearts proceeding
under venetian blinds
that have faded with the discord

Even what the blinds bar
will wind its way
into rays of accord
Newly recomposed
the day and the night
sometimes the morning
survive by just a flame
but this dawn would be everything
It broadcasts the celebratory evenings
the nights in joy
morning on its way
I would confess to this dawn a hundred times
the shaky lines of this decision
the arabesque of my flight
the field of my exhausted signs
I am on the sea brushing
against those that the noise
of the waves consoles!
Those grown from the clay of palms

And I would light neither
mourning candle
nor candle for clarity
upon the eyes of the ocean
And in no water would I
gripe about the hardship
that has caused my tears
to reverberate
There is much worse than a raft
adrift
The earth that would wreck it
The dry soil of a once-brotherly conscience
The ocean of stories
that are tragically scraped away
There is much worse than a raft
in death-throes
The earth
forgetting it's a source of life

The earth's mood
split by the same old insults
And the crying smile of an eye
that can't take in any more
its humanity damned
And us skinned
by the blow of words
scored bitterly
into our delirious bodies
And stranded in quarrels
which of the castaways speaks up?
Who explains the total loss?
Even for those who will leave tomorrow
there is much worse than a raft
adrift
This our forgetful earth
would interfere with the view of
immense seaweed tangles
like lashes at the water's edge

The earth's dour mood
this uncouth scene
whole clusters cut clean
ten a minute wiped away
lines of life swiped
from hopeful hands
But these men would never be simple winds
and their words
and their deaf prayers
Silence where his last prayer would float
Man
all of the men
what he has left to offer
is folded desperately
a single swig
on the back of that raft
I would be wind over
the ministry walls
breath murmuring beneath the tapestries
that line the hallways

I'd say happy birthday
woman-of-my-dreams
muse-of-my-awakenings
For you this bouquet of accents
bent under the weight of
crystals from my jewelry boxes
And the wave would no longer keep its shape
And the shore would no longer be sand
but electricity
Phosphorescent all the phosphor
from the zenith to its plainest angle
Optimal Geometry
This geometry of the senses
is rewritten in the length of just one
of your eyelashes
But you'd no longer understand me
And by the wish of a boat-
become-bier
shouldering into an unexpected welcome
I'd be the wind

Sometime with my sketching pencil
I'd like to whisper into her ear
what the morning breeze says
to the coastal sand
Words from the street
simple and soothing but strong
Invigorating . . .
Words made of island sand
Words that have known the pottery of the sea
Words rolling in
that whisper what the morning breeze
would say to the coastal winds . . .
And my land
our land
would laugh from shore to shore at my aspirations
My land would laugh
at this dream of fresh air

My dream
dashed a hundred times
in fate's spiraling eye
The winds like people meeting
then racing in tandem
bending the angle of each corner
Farandoles fan out in alleys
And evening's moorings loosen
The dream is dispersed in the winds
like people spread and sewn into the planet
One becomes a tempest
while others make a small headwind
Farewells sometimes celebrated like weddings
nervous joy on the docks
And people would rush would gather
would grow in resemblance
No riddle
Nature would make consonance with itself

Free of my land
then I'd exclaim innocence
an innocence made of oxygen
I offer it to myself unconditionally
to avoid vertigo
Nobody will keep me from being chaste
Innocence will perform
on an embankment that slopes endlessly away
Plied by my thirst I'd hurry there
at whim's rhythm
without likeness
without worry
without the slightest concern for elegance
I'd reimagine that fire in the ship's hold
the seasonal suicide epidemic
I'd say happy the castaways
they will be naturalized
Happy absentees
the toasts they'll receive
Haven't they lifted the elbow of that anchor
drank to the bubbles of this dream
or disinterred for us those nauseous Greek arts
the blasphemous infections
of the salacious little songs

And we'd rise on that seasick
echo
Echo where all of the secular angers
sleep off their drunkenness
The storm lodged in the ovary
of a sinking boat
We don't want
words with sores at their corners
The false requiem
no thank you
Who wants sympathies after the fact
those plaster smiles on the rescuers
of already-lost causes
We'd refuse even the caresses
that languish in the memories of those we've deserted
We'd avoid the warm hand
in a morning so blatantly cold

And the art of antiquity
would rise toward us from the bottom of the ship
Blasphemous infections
salacious little songs
And we'd rise on the echo
of the sickening sea
Echo
where the secular angers
are sleeping off their drunkenness
But where in the hollow of one's
self could this hope be reborn
that the White would not infinitely be worth
two Black as if
clefs pinned onto musical staves

The oil spill would advance
eating whole pieces of white bread
Teeth rotten the spill swallows
three-quarters of the bread
and the crumbs loosen
like a knot of intestine
The tide would slide
its slum water and seaweed
across the water's white body
Without a visa the blackened tide
is not even recognized by the sky
Convinced by the shushing waves
that all will be saved
the spill throws itself across the sea
But the bread does not like the nibbling at its torso
does not want its sides to be grazed like this
The bread begins shouting out
that it opposes such a race of teeth
Blacks on this tide have a laugh
are fed up with being fed to the sea
have a laugh as lines disappear from the rainbow
laugh at the puddle of drool on the white body
of the white bread

The spill would approach
baited by that last quarter of bread
unraveling aimlessly
the part of the bread that would sop up the oil
The black water would soon vomit that meal
Fifteen minutes
until the spill hurls in volcanic bellows
the white-bread sea
pulled in by the spill's teeth
The sea detests the oil
its ill-flavored bubbles
more murderous than piranhas
And the sea
hygienic
And the sea
ecologically minded
And the sea
reasonably burdened
aims at the bread
and pulls the trigger of its indignation
And the black sea
would go evaporating dissolving
returning to the white bread its three
stolen quarter lengths

The white bread resumes its pose in the front window
staple upon which to contemplate
not for chewing
To be consumed in the one sense but not in the other
It is a blessed bread not one sliced into
It is served according to the age-old rule
he who doesn't get a look at the menu
ends up paying the bill
The bread is served according to a plan
that has been charted by square and compass
We do not taste the darkened edges
We would not eat without precautionary speech
Wantonly
burping farting pissing
Aboard the raft you wouldn't
not with your rotten teeth
It isn't baked for laymen
This good bread
whole bread from the city

They would have needed just a sign
puff of smoke in the sky
for someone to read
alert in the eyes of the sea
panicked cries
The passengers needed just a flare
to shuttle those cries
beyond the men and women
And the voice that ricocheted
off the oil hung itself
fattened the lobe of every ear
and gradually closed the city gates
In the resonance of my dream
nationality has been distributed universally
awarded in alphabetical order
but there are three hundred and sixty-six
who have not heard their names

Then on a drop of the bitter sea
I'd demand that life itself
explain its proportions
Life would come and confess
in a voice that is tranquil
tone unimaginably calm
words softened by regret
nothing shouted
Everything is spoken from the heart
ellipses fragments strands
available to the wind
Words unwound and returning like a tune
its rustle reveals the speechlessness of grief
Life bends its knee
Its voice rises
slopes upward
It sifts through the venetian blinds
Life speaks with a straight tongue
And the words would commit
in the kind of round
held by the hands
refusing to break the circle of confession

Life's sentences hold themselves
like words linked
calling other pieces into confidence
each word grabs the shoulder strap
of the word to come
A dance initiates
Infuriated
torn from the soil
taking themselves by the hair
the sentences gather
into that coherent bouquet
always calmly in spite of the difficulty
And then this allusion to the wave
marine monster
worn on the tip of a penitent tongue
But the voice is too reedy
the word too transparent
to correspond with the field that has been provoked

Life would speak of the deaths
that could've gone another way
of this feeling in the people
who could've remained tethered
Existence's portrait in well-mixed colors
without this red too lively for those killed in war
without this sky too gray for the women still out in the waves
without this disingenuous pearl
of fortunes squeezed from those entering thirsty
The city's avenues run straight as the ocean's horizon
no possibility to swerve
Any markings are there just to attire the way

Its own wrongs wouldn't be enough anymore
Life would also admit to those of the fates
It would lift cobbles on the roads that have been off-limits
descend into misbalanced accounts
and torch the self-serving etiquette
of those keeping order over these Confessional States
Life would encamp amidst those living in the reserved anger
of fate's heavy hand:
orphans born blind
AIDS babies
albinos discarded at birth
teenagers holding meaningless diplomas
adolescents dying in childbirth
women poisoned by cancer
The cathedral begins to crumble over
at that other end of the world

But a cathedral all the same
with its altar and its organ
stained glass and icons
It clears its throat and shuts down
fate's random interludes
Life wouldn't have cried out but
would have something in its tone
like insolence or perhaps
discernment

Life reminds me also of the Djiboua Woods[1]
its towering grasses tucked beneath these skies of my breath
There where the ochre earth speaks with the aroma of the rain
sings through its flute
songs that have been dormant

*Sè ni mon-ni gougouli*
*Sè non houn hoo*[2]

*Sè ni mon-ni gougouli*
*Sè non houn hoo*

A song of frustrated love that conjures
the will to dance even against these salvos of rejection
Song of a wasted meeting
there with flowers in hand
And out in the Djiboua Woods like Stockholm syndrome
nothing ever annoys
nothing ever revolts
not the whores sucking crucifixes
nor those blind and gluttonous for their striptease
Nothing irritates
not even mosquito-y administrative attachés
not even those bed-sore from falling asleep in the throne

There in the Djiboua Woods far from the waves of my new home
nothing could ever be so normal
a dog smoking its joint
a termite nest taking its tea
a crab in fitted coat
Nothing could ever be so normal
and the seasons smoke their cigarettes
and the blubbering stars
and the flirtatious trees
Nothing but an open-armed welcome
for cyclones and thunderstorms
hail thirst and hunger
the bananas spawning offspring
the kids sniffing glue
the breath of those shepherds who want to fuck their flocks
Even the amnesic storytellers
are welcomed joyfully in a song of triumph

A rattlesnake is not like a slide trombone
any more than an ithy-
phallic statue suggests high blood pressure
Grotesque men can have names that caress
Mesmerizing words hail poisonous monsters
At the fair of false-friends enemies would be intimates
Do not expect pillow talk from dragons
Pipe organs would not soften any customs
not armed and aimed at Stalinist fascism
not at cocktail parties meant to stanch
madam Molotov's thirst
The high-pitched clucking from hens' nests
is far from the elegant cuisine
Catastrophes like these make you wonder
who has a right to be called Humanitarian

O Eritrea I'd fill the horn
New signs to banish those spells that gore fate
I'd punch the horn full of fraternal notes
a harmony to deplete the archaic songs
They are always of discord
powdery rhythmics in which verse and chorus
toss life into the pasture
into the ground into the sand
Only the sea can erase our boot prints in the clay
or destroy the sandcastle
Already determined by blood
the earth has eaten its children
The sea does not tell me
what it has done
stretching its tongue
just a few lengths from Lampedusa

The wind would fly straight from the city
rattling the bolts on shacks
and from the eye of this grim projection
I'd spill the drinks that coax
more visceral truths

And the stopwatch would lob a sun
higher than sundials can catch
this immoderate line always open to the capturing of words
The pollens of logic hatch
the word of life
from the wave that still puts seeds warm into the soil

Again on this night like the previous at Lampedusa
a nondescript heart would open
its hands to the disposable people
In the scramble and howl of outrage
its hands would be overloaded
Ten centuries of brotherhood
These hands sing Esperanto
with the solemn tone of a requiem
But the hands are nothing more than desire
led astray across shipping lanes
That heart's hands have received a mission
to carry mankind's dreams across the open sea
and here distracted by seasickness
have become immobile

And along our coasts full of remorse
these hands desire to fill their pits
as if sails now hunting after imaginary pirates
The hands are not mast or rudder
To compensate the man lost
they'd lead the way to the woman loved
or serve as jacket to swaddle the relieved child
The hands cradle the child
Not having a pied-à-terre
my drifting heart goes
to them whose breath has stopped

With abandon
and no headwind
stirrups for my feet
I'd be adventurer
wind and brother of the wind
Adventurer
My cloud of sheets is fastened
by ropes that are also
my aspirations
Moorings slack against that pasty statue of boredom
A life unveils itself
like a halo across the expanse of this instant
Always this thirst for what's ahead
this hunger for what we've left
Even our happiness
makes itself an invisible barrier from second to second

Turn the page
in every sense
so no letter is written
no line lacks luster

More than the words of sedition
more than the edicts of the tribunes
hunger harangues these crowds
Hunger entertains with tales of mountains
of marvels
Harraga[3]
*One who burns his papers*
Gamblers with memory
scratch out adolescence
redact childhood
Days at half-mast
The auto-da-fé
authored by a haggard-looking future
Any line that holds the memory of
such a vacuous adventure
These scenes would have stuck with the people
like balls of coal under their feet
ID cards hung from the neck
certificates of nationality
Hands squeezed
a police record
Or dangling feet and fist

Stop the fire brigade
their uninvited salutes
They redeem themselves by gate-crashing
Memory wrinkles its face
reading page after page of those buried days
Harraga
Hunger persuades the crowds
the hopeful who remain assembled
That which these authorities leave unsaid
the most inflammatory
words even the most agile word-parser could not shout
hunger would say it
and the war cries it
Harraga
The people forget the bile
that comes when love is purged
They shut the suitcases of hearts
swept clean through
They'd open their arms to the absence
so that the new dawn flowers
Thick hopeful cascades
Warm dream waves
Not trickles
and trickles of unfinished song

Harraga
conjugate our future
into past-perfect infinity
because the past would have us dressed
in skin woven from scars
The future must dress itself
with the sky's innocence
a beneficent gesture
offered to the hastily traced imprint of history
unlucky sketch
huffing through each day
and scattered to the four winds
There's really only this dust that is registered
to convince us that time is a virtue
Oaks die
Filaos wither
Pines decline
Palms vacillate
From now on we know that the past
it dies too

It's only to this battered hull
that the word shows its bad teeth
and in the nasty exchange laughs
about the asthmatic ships
so poorly trained to run this marathon of the sea
We'd be dashed like cigarette butts
at the bottom of this old tub
a race finished
prayers released
a tale dancing its dreams beyond the point where day drops off
Old tub
the joke about its droppings
sold at top dollar
A burial is what's offered

And there would be five hundred such pieces of shit
walking all the weight of their fleshless bodies
Five hundred carrying prayers
of the cross and the crescent in their hearts
Dream signals scrambled
They'd be five hundred women and men
then one would take out its modeling clay
and another a slate
she'd straighten the sticks of chalk in her blouse pocket
Over there one says mom
she'd know all the letters
she'd know how to write the word life
if that's what God wants
And if God doesn't want it?
Mama slaps her

Because mama holds her humanities dear
she'd not make them less superstitious
knowing the gods
their animal quarrels
and their inhuman passions
She knows the loves of Zeus and of Terra Mater
in her own body
And of Laërtes and Anticlea
and of Ulysses's quest on this same Mediterranean
which guards the memory of those times in its dance
She'd nearly see Sirens giggling on the bow of this raft
The Cyclops
Charybdis and Scylla
Circe the enchantress
and wily Eurylochus too
Mama is no racist
but she knows that the Nereids
are Somalian
The Oceanids Eritrean
Charybdis and Scylla Malian
For sure
Polyphemus the Cyclops
is Nigerian

The abundance of any god
would fall harmlessly on these five hundred
heads rolled at the will of the wind
Many hearts address the sky
send some easy winds
The book of life would be written in a mathematical language
Brows wrinkle
refiguring the invoice for these last days
Waiting for the hour of departure
the puffy faces explain how to divide a ration
how much to share between younger children
an equation with multiple unknowns
In this exercise you multiply the circles under your eyes
Here the number would be more real than ever
This precise and faulty subtraction
imposes five hundred less
three hundred and sixty-six
Only the crane of Lampedusa has discovered the actual answer

The wave of memories crashes inside me
it would be Sunday
Through candles
and fluttery things
God whispers a charming song
Somewhere from the infatuated hive of this chapter
I desire to say "I love you"
but each word lists on
the scale of my rupturing heart
I would be joined then
in the watertight silence
because honestly
since the day before my dear
I am no longer of flesh
on the back of the raft
In the water I would inhabit
the first floor of a six-floored ocean

I'd live a quiet life with my two cats
Trains of water would die out
idle in the striking harbor
The oldest of the city would only know
that I come and go with this basket of provisions in hand
Market days I pull on an old woolen shawl
even under this marine sun
I separate myself from the material begrudgingly
It gives me the air of a Bedouin
and in certain places of the market the shawl
muffles the stench of fish rotting

The newcomer in this water finds
the deteriorated products we put on sale
incongruous
But all would know that in this city
household goods are available
dishes of rotten fish served fresh
The marine wind is such that each soul
lives according to the drift

At times my dream would turn narrow
beating the earth's head
into some glacial era
crowning it with hypothermia
lakes rigid as the devil's dick
A stock exchange pinching every last drop of the earth's assets
Fruits become rare shivering
at angles in the icy branches
The boats are returning to the Île de Gorée[4]
loving it to death
each stone
every leaf
every piece of baobab bark in Dakar
My dream would be narrow
I would close it

And even a roiling sea
isn't too much if you have
the kiss of the sun against your cheek
If the wave coughs
that's not too much to endure
holding yourself against the chest of the wind
That wave would dance the waltz of buried wishes
The wave would rock the silent tongues in its bed
So many departures
so many arrivals
But the wave would also know the happiness of the survivors
their wait in the alpine summit of Lukmanier Pass
They are the shivering stockage of a land that fears
the fears of this other
who like unfortunate Ulysses
is without papers

The Trojan War as it would've really happened
Received by a coastguard armed to the teeth
Ulysses would be taken aback
Having roamed under too many suns
he would have lost his race to the hunt
Ulysses would have the countenance of Soumangourou Kanté[5]
Some would take him for Dieudonné Mbala Mbala[6]
which could be good for Ulysses
The misfortune is that he has arrived with the Boat people
There is really no way forward
Not boot-stomping and bombastic
not club-footed
He has no Trojan horse
no secret weapon in the hull of his ship
The guard puts a boot on the rail:
Where do you come from and where do you plan to go
Ulysses at first naturally avoids the question
I search in the haystack of your gaze
*La liberté*
*l'égalité* and
*la fraternité*
The coastguard looking him in the eye
is not missing with his retort: You could also
go look for these in Haiti
if you want

*Les sans papiers*
are lacking not only their papers
they lack themselves
The man the woman the child
they were before becoming ship rats
released at the base of the Alps
where one-without-papers
has no rights
He owes even the right to breathe
And those who attend the funerals
of accomplices strewn around Lampedusa
will be detained

October 3
The slow vessels carrying autumn's violators
crunch the dock
in this monotonous stretch
Mulling over how I am blamed
and how I am baited
I remember
the dog days
and implore
let me go out ahead of those dreams
I was led to this sand
October 3
Three more months until a new year
three days from a new age
my past sufferings disappear between my hands
October 3
Three and ten
Thirty
Thirty and ten
Three hundred
Three hundred sixty-six

The boat offered in flames held women
The water and the fire opposite elements
accomplices as death spread itself
Death doesn't spare the women
not even those it has so recently let pass
they clutch their babies
The fire could have at least been sensitive to them
intimates of the hearth
and of water from the beginning of time
Death would have recognized
the fire's catchy gossip
but in the sea
as in death
this old war against the women plays out completely
This October 3
their bodies float between the water and the flames

The same lovely war
The sea as is death
The battered hull would begin to unflap
its beautiful mouth of statistics
This sea of endemic wreckage
Some cry seventeen thousand deaths in twenty years
others only three thousand
as if each corpse in this Mediterranean
was not excessive
As if every child drowned
every sputtering hope
every excised dream
not too much on that long nightmare of ocean
The sea asked only to be contemplated
to ease the anxiety of the separations
to erase the anguish of irreplaceable lovers
To be nothing more than an avenue
open to our human hope

In leaving Libya in rags
the fishermen-guides arrive already
short of the beyond
indistinguishable from any other SOS
The fever for their boats makes them mad
for money crumpled deep in the pockets
of these young nafkas[7]
It doesn't look good but in order to leave the dry lands
to be well away from words that lance the heart
far from the shootings that orchestrate the hours
far from the rapes that inseminate this troubled century
it is necessary
Message corked
that tells the world of a thirst for the day after tomorrow
recolored with pencils
blue for the generosities of the sea
pink for the forthcoming life
and the rainbow for all the happiness
of that unreleased horizon

The ship's bridge would be compromised
wet to the neck with fuel
an agreement made with the other shore
To connect
this is the sacred role of the bridge
its long-standing commitment
But the fuel
it has constructed a span
that is gone as soon as the spark is supplied
A strand of gloom ignites to transform the Mediterranean
In Acheron
fire
fire from all directions
The bridge collapses under the weight of flames and people

Before the spark
sets the shoreline blazing
the rashness of men has already
misread the future
And the psalms
And the suras
Appetites would do the rest
Cross and crescent
Blades flash over the infirmary
bed of a sallow country
Not a single night escapes
being splayed by those weapons
Day in day out eyes gouged
The men design
their own differences
bagged then boxed
Lifting the cargo through its bubbles
the crane saw no label
on the orthodox back
nor on the Sunni torso

A cat with no other role
in life than to be a tomcat
would decide to play his wild card role
quite naturally
quite practically
He'd bathe
stand erect
At attention he'd wait for the slightest intruder
rule book in hand
He'd have the reflex and good luck to spy
even the mouse sneaking through the sky
at the speed of light
He'd take its breath
swish it between his cheeks
then whistle breath and soul
out through that tunnel
and smoke would rise would rise
then rise as if from fevering branches
The cat would stick him with an infraction for misbehavior
The mouse would take offense at it
but this tomcat would be a cat
with no other purpose
than to be the mistigris
quite naturally
quite practically

The men play cat and mouse with people's lives
a geometrically variable well-being
when we all well know
that their map of goods excludes the good-of-all
excludes actual bodies
Any belief that this evil is vanquished
in crossing from one side of the Pyrenees to the other
is misbegotten
I'd be an ocean of sand
with its storms and its dunes
selectively indignant
The men nevertheless remain
waterlogged and
slogging through the illusion of their differences

They are of the same vineyard
though a vintage that obscures its traces
in the fuss over identity
Nothing
No pinch of powder
if it is not the dust of flight
in their anxiety to avoid this other

Don't lose sight of the people of Lampedusa
with whom we've shared beds
We're from the same mountains
same foam
Don't forget that our waves
dump us from the same sack
same surf
Father-shores
and mother-sea in unison

The ground is nothing but the sea's fossil
trace of the oceanic
wanting to remain anonymous
Deep in its throat each sea shifts a tongue of crust
makes itself enigmatic to the mother tongues
Mare Nostrum[8]
where people try to relight
the fire of a brotherhood smothered by sandstorms
Siblings risk their gains
out on the surface of the sea again
beautifully optimistic
that this is not just another knife in the back

We'd be five sheets of seaweed
there in the anger of one apocalyptic night
wrapping the tears of our women
the doubts of our mothers
the suffering of our daughters
in fragile promises

Insulin to the mother
to calm her hostile flood of sugars
The other letting her betrothed go
celebrating an Easter farewell
The third lost
to a blur in the vision of that malarial girl
sobbing on departure day
A Barbie doll and pretty plates
for Yohada at Christmas
The last two their heads are thick with insomnia

Already immense sheets float in the water
the water lashes along the rocks of Lampedusa
We harvested more than three hundred

At Christmas, Yohada did not have her doll

More than six hundred meters
Mere cable lengths until finally a quiet home
walls peering back from the horizon
After the ocean's wild swells
hardly more than six hundred meters
and back far back in the sands of Africa
a girl nearly gets her fancy plates
Six hundred more meters
and back far back in the sands of Africa
a mother would begin to lift her head again
More than six hundred meters
and far back in the sands of Africa
a Marabout swaggers
falling through the doors of the dream
The plates do not come
The mother keeps her head bowed
The Marabout has changed the state of residence

I went to town to find blue ink
for my jaundice-drugged forest
The sprawling orchard of my faith
twisted into tubs on pallets
I went when the night and the daytime
were hand-in-hand
between dog and wolf
The watercolor of their winds overlapping
so that it is friendship that instructs the one hand
to draw in the other of day
The seasons need to make their peace
It's necessary that the solstices have done their shopping at the same stalls
The day would have been a mango transplanted
its orange skin licking the flesh of an apple
A new material would spin the cotton of new adventures
and the language that it speaks
would turn its maxims seven times in the palace of dawn

Now time would reveal
its callipygian pose
would carry its fine round ass
from the storehouses that keep its tattoos cool
too proud of those tints
inherited from the big bang
and the stretch-marked memory it considers a chapel
in the rearview mirror

Time needs to air some dirty laundry
to be exposed just as we are on these lines
It must mix yolks and whites before it breaks the shell
Then engender the black
Conceive the white
Dream the green and the blue
Birth the ochre
The blue and the orange
with no cracks

Lampedusa
I'll be breath for your
early breeze
wind savoring each riddle the world offers
In the birds taking flight
from these literary circles
in a flurry of wings
crossing the borders
The east's rising wind
The comforting west wind
Wind this day wind tomorrow lifting the blinds
And I would rile you often
The voice of the wind
sets out ahead like this

Shrouded within its verb
the voice
approaches the shores
The untraceable voice
addresses the face of the violent sky
For sale
the wish of rains to come
those from the high lands and that
of the valley seated alone at its table
Wind at the hours of the grape harvest
Wind in the drunken night
And the true wind
from the cardinal directions
of the north
of the south
They air the secrets of their geographies
in the four far corners of this field
lost in sails

At the back of the raft
I invent a city
dependable as a diurnal tale
A city that fills all of our hopes with the scent of lemon
We'd dream passionately about this city
The thirst of its travelers sticking in its long mane
On its docks one thousand workers
build the dreams they would step into
youthfully extravagant
I would be there
a centenary stalactite where the sand
is dredged
its stela sparkling in the center of my words
The tower of a convoluted world
earth crammed shoulder to shoulder
upholder
and the trowel and the ember of revolts
the accent of subversion
This taste of the horizon hoisted is unique
Here where the latitudes repeat
I know the price
the real price of our sentence
how much blood it costs to dance on these scaffolds
with trowel in hand

I'd be a man defying the fence
that's electric with hate
I'd sell my newspapers at the traffic lights
Laughter
and she sits comfortably in the back of a speeding car
She lowers the window
and recognizing one another instantly
we would start the world over
Life would quickly weave its raffia canvas
The shouts from the streets would change
Me tired of selling newspapers
of filling the air with my voice
Cries to her would offer nothing
but this silence begins to make sense

Sometimes it would be an order
that is already not an order
A prayer
An order that would keep this firm tone of injunction
but it would be wet to the neck
complicit
Then the word itself would mix in the throat

I'd know the seditious words
The signs of the thunderstorm
are so clear in poorly lit districts
those nervous atmospheres
nativities without their saviors
Christmas where the construction workers' daughters
find an ear of corn
like the deflated doll
in dreams that have already been taken down
I'd also know nights where the groin of day
stretches awake
intersections of burning tires faces of kaolin and coal
I'd know the end of these closed meetings of the minds
I'd know the inevitability of a day where nothing goes wrong
the mornings of hands willingly held
dawns of church bells and calls-to-prayer
that finally include the sacred rumor
just in from the jungle

# NOTES

1. Djiboua literally means "on the path of the panther" in Dida, which is the poet's first language. Djiboua is the symbolic name of the city of Divo, the poet's city of origin, in the Ivory Coast.
2. The text is in Dida and translates as: "You hurt me in a way that I would never expect from you."
3. *Harraga* is an Arabic word that means "the burners" or "those who burn" and refers to the North Africans who burn their identity papers in an effort to seek asylum in Europe. For many, the migration involves secretly boating to European-controlled islands such as Lampedusa.
4. Île de Gorée is an island off the coast of Dakar, Senegal. The island was one of the earliest European settlements in Africa and was used as a trading post by the various European nations that took possession of it. The island is depicted as a point of departure for slaves during the period of Atlantic slave trade and with its "House of Slaves" serves as a prominent memorial site.
5. Soumangourou Kanté was a thirteenth-century king of the Sosso people. As the Ghana Empire fell, Kanté seized its capital and then several neighboring states. In the Mandinka state (what is now Mali), prince Sundiata Keita created a coalition and defeated Kanté. This is recounted in Mali's national epic, which portrays Kanté as a sorcerer-king. After being shot by an arrow with a white rooster crest on it—the only weapon to which he is vulnerable—Kanté flees into the mountains. While Ulysses had a bow only he could draw, Kanté owned a musical instrument, the balafon, that had magical powers.
6. Dieudonné Mbala Mbala is a French comedian. His father was Cameroonian and his mother was a white French woman. He began his career as part of a duo in which he and his Jewish partner exchanged racist jokes. Dieudonné is often charged with anti-Semitism and inciting hate. France banned him from performing in 2014,

but for many young first or second generation immigrants, especially those who have come from Africa, attempts to censor Dieudonné have added to his appeal. Dieudonné contrasts himself with Charlie Hebdo.

7. Nafka is slang for a person from Eritrea. It is the name of the town in which Eritrean independence fighters headquartered their resistance to Ethiopia during the Eritrean War of Independence, which ended in 1991. The nafka is also the Eritrean currency.

8. *Mare nostrum* was the Roman name for the Mediterranean Sea, meaning "our sea" in Latin. It was the name for an Italian government sea rescue operation initiated in late 2013 as a response to this shipwreck at Lampedusa. Operation Mare Nostrum was meant to address increased migration from Africa and the Middle East. Without funding from the European Union the yearlong operation ended and was replaced by Operation Triton. Run by the EU's border security agency, Triton is a much smaller operation focused on policing rather than lifesaving.

IN THE AFRICAN POETRY BOOK SERIES

*After the Ceremonies:*
*New and Selected Poems*
Ama Ata Aidoo
Edited and with a foreword
by Helen Yitah

*The Promise of Hope: New and*
*Selected Poems, 1964–2013*
Kofi Awoonor
Edited and with an introduction
by Kofi Anyidoho

*The January Children*
Safia Elhillo

*Madman at Kilifi*
Clifton Gachagua

*Think of Lampedusa*
Josué Guébo
Translated by Todd Fredson
Introduction by John Keene

*Beating the Graves*
Tsitsi Ella Jaji

*Gabriel Okara: Collected Poems*
Gabriel Okara
Edited and with an introduction
by Brenda Marie Osbey

*The Kitchen-Dweller's Testimony*
Ladan Osman

*Fuchsia*
Mahtem Shiferraw

*In a Language That You Know*
Len Verwey

*Logotherapy*
Mukoma Wa Ngugi

*When the Wanderers Come Home*
Patricia Jabbeh Wesley

*Seven New Generation African Poets:*
*A Chapbook Box Set*
Edited by Kwame Dawes
and Chris Abani
(Slapering Hol)

*Eight New-Generation African Poets:*
*A Chapbook Box Set*
Edited by Kwame Dawes
and Chris Abani
(Akashic Books)

*New-Generation African Poets:*
*A Chapbook Box Set (Tatu)*
Edited by Kwame Dawes
and Chris Abani
(Akashic Books)

*New-Generation African Poets:*
*A Chapbook Box Set (Nne)*
Edited by Kwame Dawes
and Chris Abani
(Akashic Books)

To order or obtain more information on these or other University of Nebraska Press titles, visit nebraskapress.unl.edu. For more information about the African Poetry Book Series, visit africanpoetrybf.unl.edu.

Lightning Source UK Ltd.
Milton Keynes UK
UKOW01f0018170817
307469UK00001B/22/P